CHART HITS NOW!

EASY F
IMPOS...
easy piano
...PLUS 11 MORE TOP HITS

CW00722223

WISE PUBLICATIONS
part of The Music Sales Group
London / New York / Paris / Sydney / Copenhagen / Berlin / Madrid / Hong Kong / Tokyo

Published by
Wise Publications
14-15 Berners Street, London W1T 3LJ, UK.

Exclusive Distributors:

Music Sales Limited
Distribution Centre, Newmarket Road,
Bury St Edmunds, Suffolk IP33 3YB, UK.

Music Sales Pty Limited
Units 3-4, 17 Willfox Street, Condell Park
NSW 2200, Australia.

Order No. AM1006302
ISBN: 978-1-78305-002-4
This book © Copyright 2013 Wise Publications,
a division of Music Sales Limited.

Edited by Jenni Norey.
Arrangements and engravings supplied by Camden Music Services.

Printed in the EU.

Your Guarantee of Quality:
As publishers, we strive to produce every book
to the highest commercial standards.
This book has been carefully designed to minimise awkward page turns
and to make playing from it a real pleasure.
Particular care has been given to specifying acid-free, neutral-sized paper
made from pulps which have not been elemental chlorine bleached.
This pulp is from farmed sustainable forests and was produced
with special regard for the environment.
Throughout, the printing and binding have been planned to ensure a sturdy,
attractive publication which should give years of enjoyment.
If your copy fails to meet our high standards, please inform us
and we will gladly replace it.

www.musicsales.com

BENEATH YOUR BEAUTIFUL • LABRINTH FEAT. EMELI SANDÉ • 4

CANDY • ROBBIE WILLIAMS • 10

HALF OF ME • RIHANNA • 20

HE AIN'T HEAVY, HE'S MY BROTHER • JUSTICE COLLECTIVE • 15

HO HEY • THE LUMINEERS • 26

IMPOSSIBLE • JAMES ARTHUR • 36

LITTLE THINGS • ONE DIRECTION • 31

LOCKED OUT OF HEAVEN • BRUNO MARS • 40

LOVEBIRD • LEONA LEWIS • 44

ONE MORE NIGHT • MAROON 5 • 49

SKYFALL • ADELE • 54

TROUBLEMAKER • OLLY MURS FEAT. FLO RIDA • 59

Beneath Your Beautiful

Words & Music by Timothy McKenzie, Mike Posner
& Emeli Sandé

8

Candy

Words & Music by Robbie Williams, Gary Barlow
& Terje Olsen

1. I was there to wit - ness__ Can - dice - 's in - ner bus - 'ness.__ She
2. Ring a ring of ro - ses__ who - ev - er gets the clo - sest.__ She

wants the boys to no - tice__ her rain - bows and her po - nies.__ She was ed - u - ca - ted__ but
comes and she goes as__ the war of__ the ro - ses.__ Moth - er was a vic - tim.__

could not count to ten now she got lots of diff - 'rent hor - ses by
Fa - ther beat the sys - tem__ by mov - ing bricks to Brix - ton and

Hey! Ho! Here she go. Ei - ther a lit - tle too loud or a lit - tle too close. With a

hur - ri - cane___ at the back of her throat she thinks she's made of can - dy.___

1.

2.

Li - ber - ate___ your___

doing it___ for? What are you doing it___ for? What are you

doing it___ for? What are you doing it___ for?

1, 3. Hey! Ho! Here she go. Ei - ther a lit - tle too high or a lit - tle too low. With no___
2, 4. Hey! Ho! Here she go. Ei - ther a lit - tle too loud or a lit - tle too close. With a

___ self es - teem and ver - ti - go 'cause she thinks she's made of can - dy.___
hur - ri - cane___ at the back of her throat

1-3.

thinks she's made of can - dy.___

4.

thinks she's made of can - dy.___

14

He Ain't Heavy, He's My Brother

Words & Music by Bob Russell & Robert William Scott

Half Of Me

Words & Music by Mikkel Eriksen, Tor Erik Hermansen,
Shahid Khan & Emeli Sandé

in. You saw me on a te-le-vi - sion,

saw me on a te-le-vi-sion, but that's just the half of it.

Yeah, you saw the half of it.

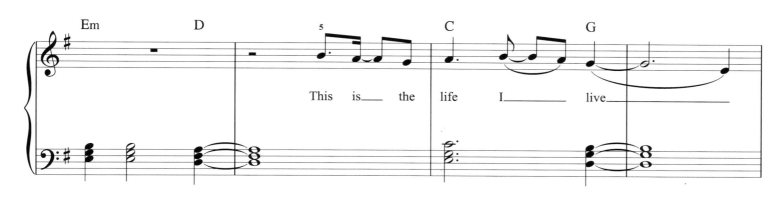

This is the life I live

24

And that's just_ the half of_ it.

You saw_ the half of_ it.

Yeah, this is_ the life I_ live_ and that's just_ the

half of_ it. Yeah, you saw_ the

You saw me on a te-le-vi - sion,_ saw me on a te-le-vi-sion._

Ho Hey

Words & Music by Jeremy Fraites & Wesley Schultz

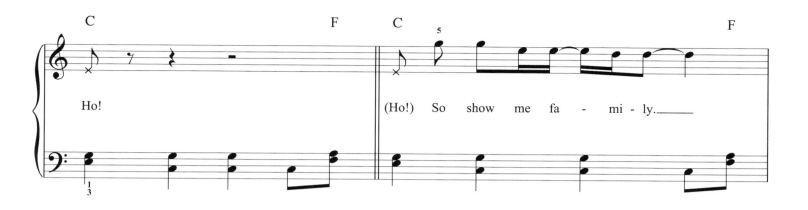

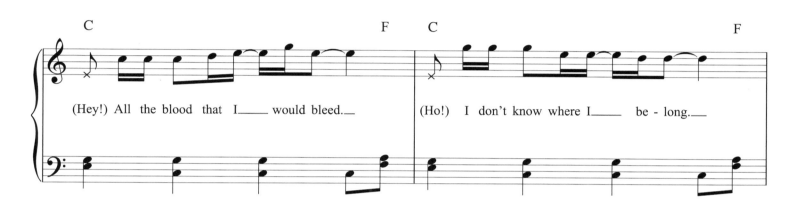

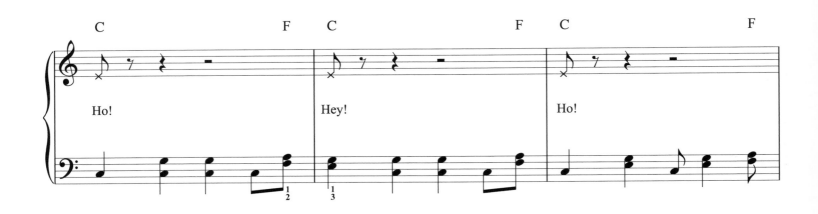

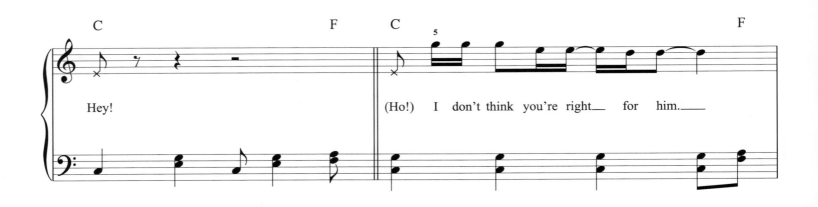

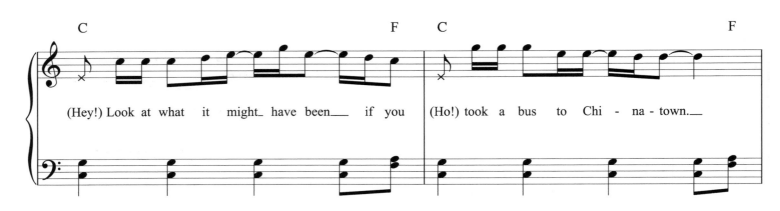

28

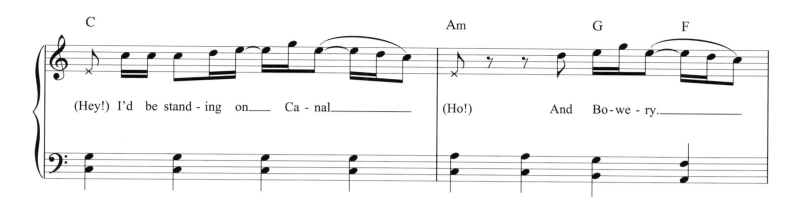

(Hey!) I'd be stand-ing on___ Ca-nal_____ (Ho!) And Bo-we-ry._____

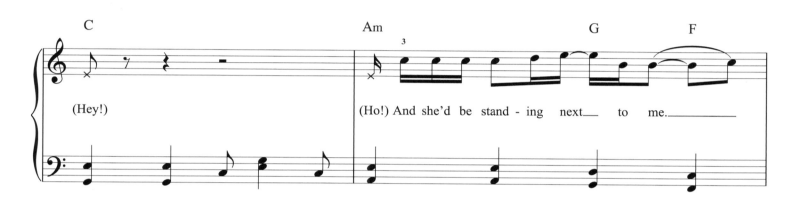

(Hey!) (Ho!) And she'd be stand-ing next___ to me._____

(Hey! Two, three...) I be-long with you, you be-long with me you're my___ sweet-

- heart___ I be-long with you, you be-long with me you're my___ sweet - heart._

29

Little Things

Words & Music by Ed Sheeran & Fiona Bevan

32

Impossible

Words & Music by Arnthor Birgisson & Ina Wroldsen

-ble,_____ im - pos - si - ble,_____ im - pos - si - ble.

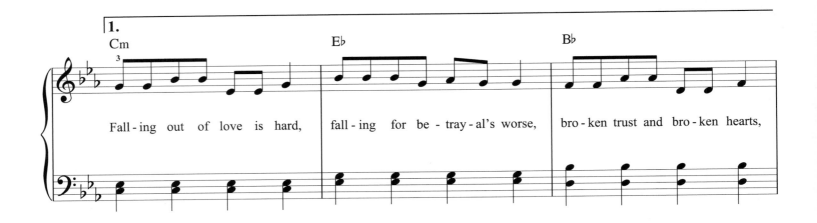

Fall - ing out of love is hard, fall - ing for be - tray - al's worse, bro - ken trust and bro - ken hearts,

I know.___ I know__ think - ing all you need is there, build - ing faith on love and words,

emp - ty prom - is - es will wear, I know,___ I know. And now when all is done there is noth - ing to

Locked Out Of Heaven

Words & Music by Ari Levine, Philip Lawrence
& Peter Hernandez

Lovebird

Words & Music by Lukasz Gottwald, Bonnie McKee
& Joshua Coleman

One More Night

Words & Music by Savan Kotecha, Adam Levine,
Martin Max & Johan Schuster

2.

D   Am   Em

Ooh,   ooh ooh ooh   ooh   ooh   ooh   ooh.__

D   Am   Em

__ Yeah, ba - by give me one   more__ night.   Ooh,   ooh ooh ooh   ooh   ooh   ooh   ooh.__

1.

D   Am

__ Yeah, ba - by give me one   more__ night.

2.

D   Am

__   But

Em   D   Am⁷

ba - by, there you go a - gain, there you go a - gain,   mak - ing me love you.   Yeah,

Em   D   Am⁷

I stopped us - ing my head, us - ing my head,   let it all go.____   Got

52

Skyfall

Words & Music by Paul Epworth & Adele Adkins

Troublemaker

Words & Music by Stephen Robson, Claude Kelly,
Olly Murs & Flo Rida

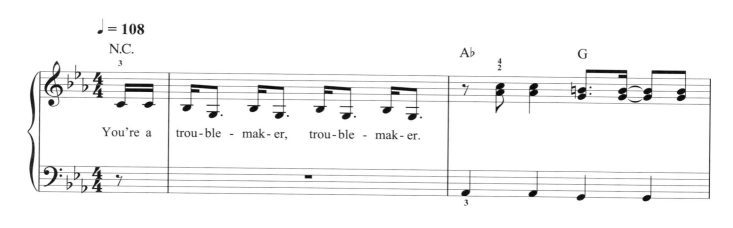

You're a trou-ble - mak- er, trou-ble - mak- er.

Spoken: You ain't noth-ing but a trou-ble-mak- er, girl.

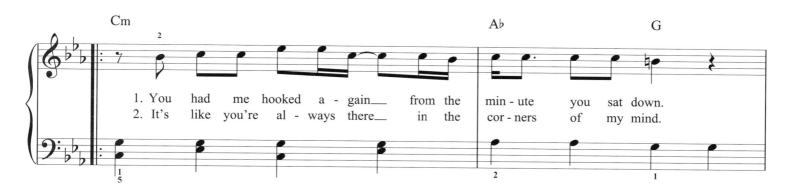

1. You had me hooked a - gain___ from the min - ute you sat down.
2. It's like you're al - ways there___ in the cor - ners of my mind.

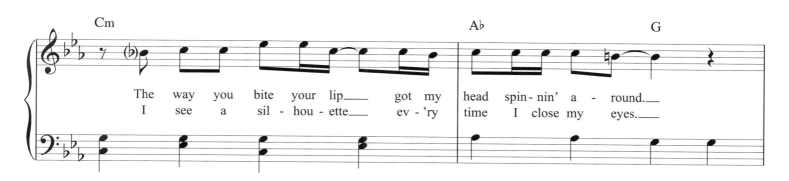

The way you bite your lip___ got my head spin-nin' a - round.___
I see a sil - hou - ette___ ev - 'ry time I close my eyes.___

123456789

Bringing you the words and the music

All the latest music in print... rock & pop plus jazz, blues, country, classical and the best in West End show scores.

- Books to match your favourite CDs.

- Book-and-CD titles with high quality backing tracks for you to play along to. Now you can play guitar or piano with your favourite artist... or simply sing along!

- Audition songbooks with CD backing tracks for both male and female singers for all those with stars in their eyes.

- Can't read music? No problem, you can still play all the hits with our wide range of chord songbooks.

- Check out our range of instrumental tutorial titles, taking you from novice to expert in no time at all!

- Musical show scores include *The Phantom Of The Opera*, *Les Misérables*, *Mamma Mia* and many more hit productions.

- DVD master classes featuring the techniques of top artists.

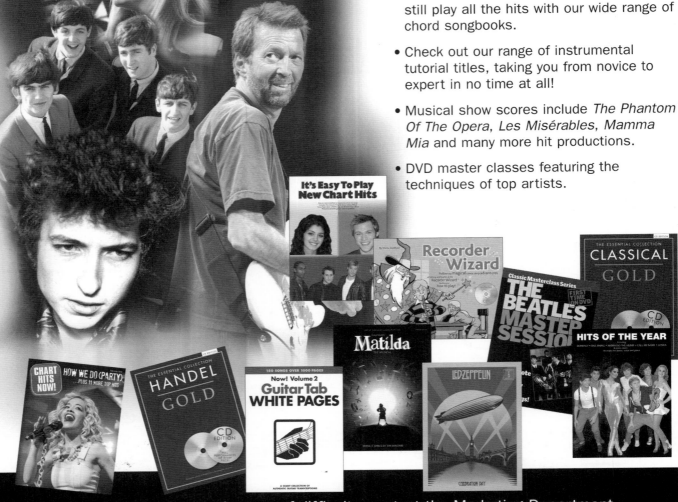

Visit your local music shop or, in case of difficulty, contact the Marketing Department, Music Sales Limited, Newmarket Road, Bury St Edmunds, Suffolk, IP33 3YB, UK
marketing@musicsales.co.uk